International E
Biol
Optic
Neurobiology and Behaviour

Introduction

Welcome to the International Baccalaureate Neurobiology and Behaviour Revision Guide.

The layout is similar to the main guide with the key points highlighted and summarised. Once again there are numerous revision questions within the text.

Statements are in pale blue boxes.

Statement

There are very few definitions in the Options and so these have been incorporated in the text in pink boxes.

Definition

In the top right hand corner of the page are green boxes that give the heading for that sub division of the Option.

Stimulus and Response

I am grateful to my students who provided helpful advice on the text and diagrams. Once again I would greatly value any feedback on this revision guide so that later editions can continue to help students throughout the world. Please feel free to email me at Oxford Study Courses – osc@osc-ib.com.

Ashby Merson-Davies.

Option E

Neurobiology and Behaviour

Core Material

❖ Stimulus and Response

Stimulus
A change in the internal or external environment that is detected by a receptor and causes a response.

Response
A change in an organism as a result of a stimulus.

Reflex
A rapid and unconscious response to a stimulus.

Animal Response to Stimuli

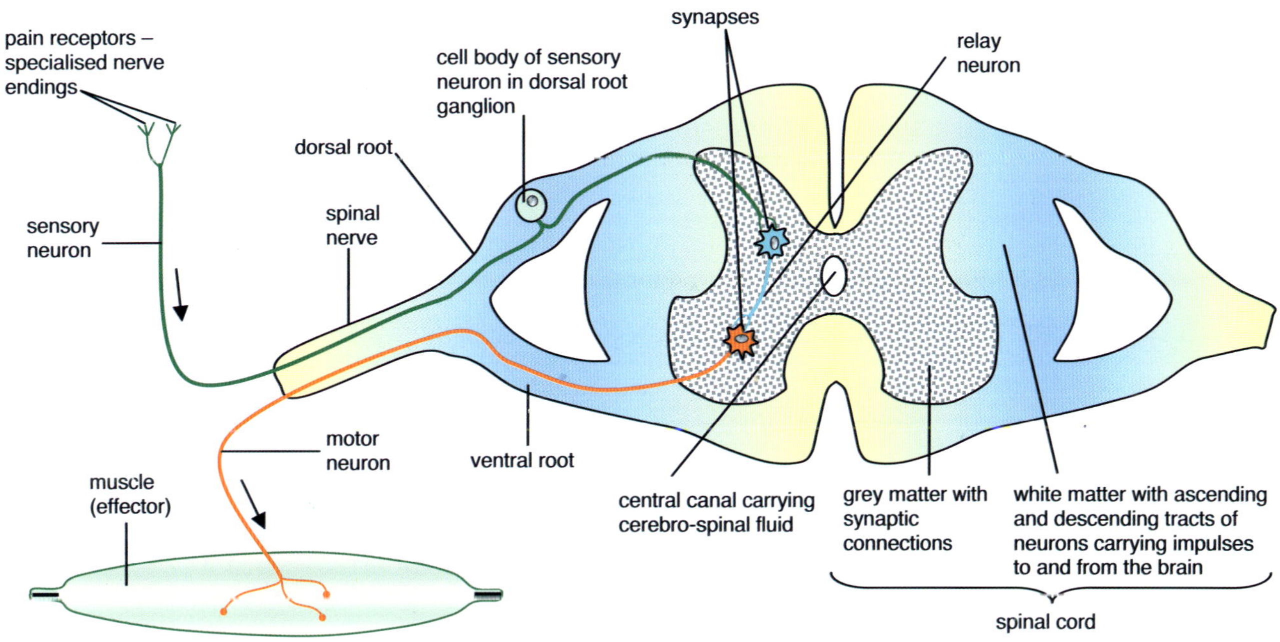

Key components

- ➢ **Receptor**
  - Specialised cell or nerve ending;
  - Detects a specific stimulus;
  - Detects internal and external stimuli.
- ➢ **Sensory neuron**
  - Carries nerve impulses from the receptor to the central nervous system.
- ➢ **Relay neuron**
  - Carries nerve impulses from the sensory to the motor neuron;
  - Links up with other relay neurons to carry information up and down the spinal cord, eg to the memory centres of the brain.
- ➢ **Motor neuron**
  - Carries nerve impulses from the central nervous system to the effector.
- ➢ **Synapses**
  - Connect neurons together;
  - Control how the information is passed from one neuron to the next;
  - Uses chemicals called neurotransmitters.
- ➢ **Effector**
  - Carries out a response to the stimulus.

The Role of Natural Selection in Response

Key points

- Responses may increase survival and reproduction;
- Responses show adaptive significance by improving fitness;
- Fitness is the genetic contribution of an individual to later generations;
- Natural selection acts on differences that have a genetic basis;
- Response patterns that improve fitness get passed on to offspring. (Darwinian principle).

Examples of Responses

Egg laying

- The Blue tit, *Cyanistes caeruleus*, and the Great tit, *Parus major*, are birds commonly found through Great Britain and other parts of Europe;
- They feed mainly on insects;
- As temperatures have risen insects are appearing earlier in spring;
- Both species have responded by breeding earlier in the year as shown by egg laying data in the tables and graphs below.

Blue tit, *Cyanistes caeruleus*.

Variable	Period (yrs)	Years	Mean annual sample	Trend	Modelled in first year	Modelled in 2005	Change
Clutch size	37	1968-2005	131	Linear decline	9.41 eggs	8.57 eggs	-8.9%
Brood size	37	1968-2005	220	Curvilinear	8.04 chicks	7.01 chicks	-12.7%
Laying date	**37**	**1968-2005**	**173**	**Linear decline**	**May 3**	**Apr 26**	**- 7 days**

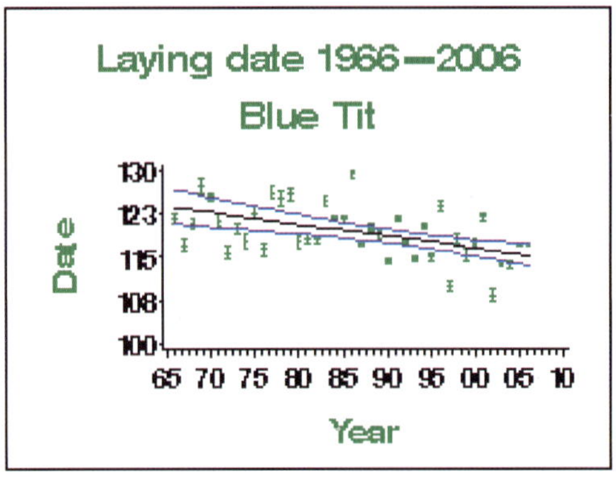

Photo George H Higginbotham

Baillie, S.R., Marchant, J.H., Crick, H.Q.P., Noble, D.G., Balmer, D.E., Barimore, C., Coombes, R.H., Downie, I.S., Freeman, S.N., Joys, A.C., Leech, D.I., Raven, M.J., Robinson, R.A. & Thewlis, R.M. (2007) Breeding Birds in the Wider Countryside: their conservation status 2007. BTO Research Report No. 487. BTO.

Great tit, *Parus major*

Variable	Period (yrs)	Years	Mean annual sample	Trend	Predicted in first year	Predicted in last year	Change
Clutch size	34	1968-2002	92	Linear decline	8.23 eggs	7.61 eggs	-0.62 eggs
Brood size	34	1968-2002	158	Linear decline	7.44 chicks	6.56 chicks	-0.88 chicks
Laying date	34	1968-2002	113	Curvilinear	day 121	day 113	-8 days

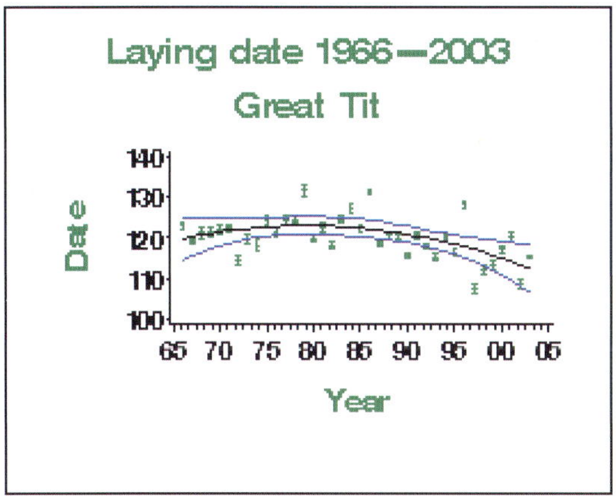

Photo Tommy Holden

Baillie, S.R., Marchant, J.H., Crick, H.Q.P., Noble, D.G., Balmer, D.E., Beaven, L.P., Coombes, R.H., Downie, I.S., Freeman, S.N., Joys, A.C., Leech, D.I., Raven, M.J., Robinson, R.A. and Thewlis, R.M. (2005) Breeding Birds in the Wider Countryside: their conservation status 2004. BTO Research Report No. 385. BTO, Thetford.

The data tables, graphs and photos for both species have been reproduced by kind permission of the British Trust for Ornithology.

Migration

This is movement over long distances.

The bird *Sylvia atricapilla* or Blackcap

- Breeds over most of Europe;
- German blackcaps normally migrate southwest to over-winter in the western Mediterranean;
- Rising winter temperatures in the UK increased food supplies.
- More birds are now found in the UK during the winter months but ringing studies show that they bred in Germany;
- Over-wintering birds were captured in the UK and in the western Mediterranean, taken to Germany and bred over two seasons;
- Thus all birds had the same environmental cues;
- Observations on migration behaviour in captivity showed the birds would fly in a direction that took them to their expected over-wintering region;
- This shows that the direction of migration is genetically programmed;
- Birds that do not fly as far south to over-winter can get back to the breeding grounds sooner and with less expenditure of energy;
- This will give them a selective advantage over those birds that have to return from further south;

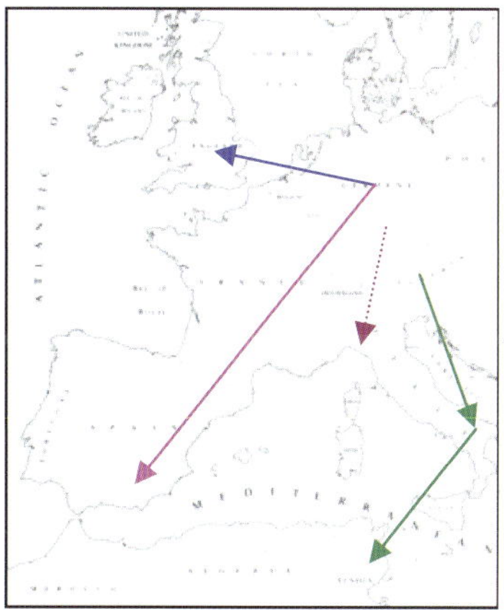

- Birds from Austria tended to fly southeast to the eastern Mediterranean and then south to over-winter in eastern Africa;
- Cross-breeding the Austrian and German birds produced offspring that tended to fly in a direction between those of the parent populations;
- This is further evidence that migration direction is genetically controlled.

Stimulus and Response

Define stimulus.

Define response.

Define reflex.

Label the diagram in the 14 places indicated.

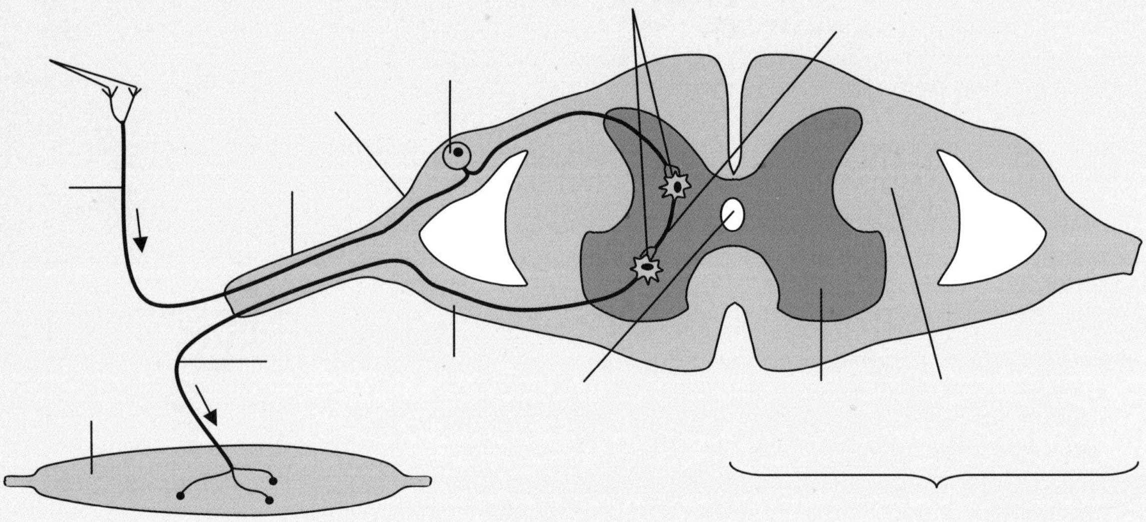

Use one example to illustrate how animal response is affected by natural selection.

❖ Perception of Stimuli

	Mechanoreceptors	Chemoreceptors	Thermoreceptors	Photoreceptors
Stimulus	Mechanical movement	Chemicals	Temperature	Light
Types	Stretch receptors in muscles are used to position muscles in co-ordinated movements.	Taste and smell receptors on the tongue and in the nose	Hypothalamus measures temperature of blood for temperature homeostasis.	Rods and cones in the retina.

The Human Eye

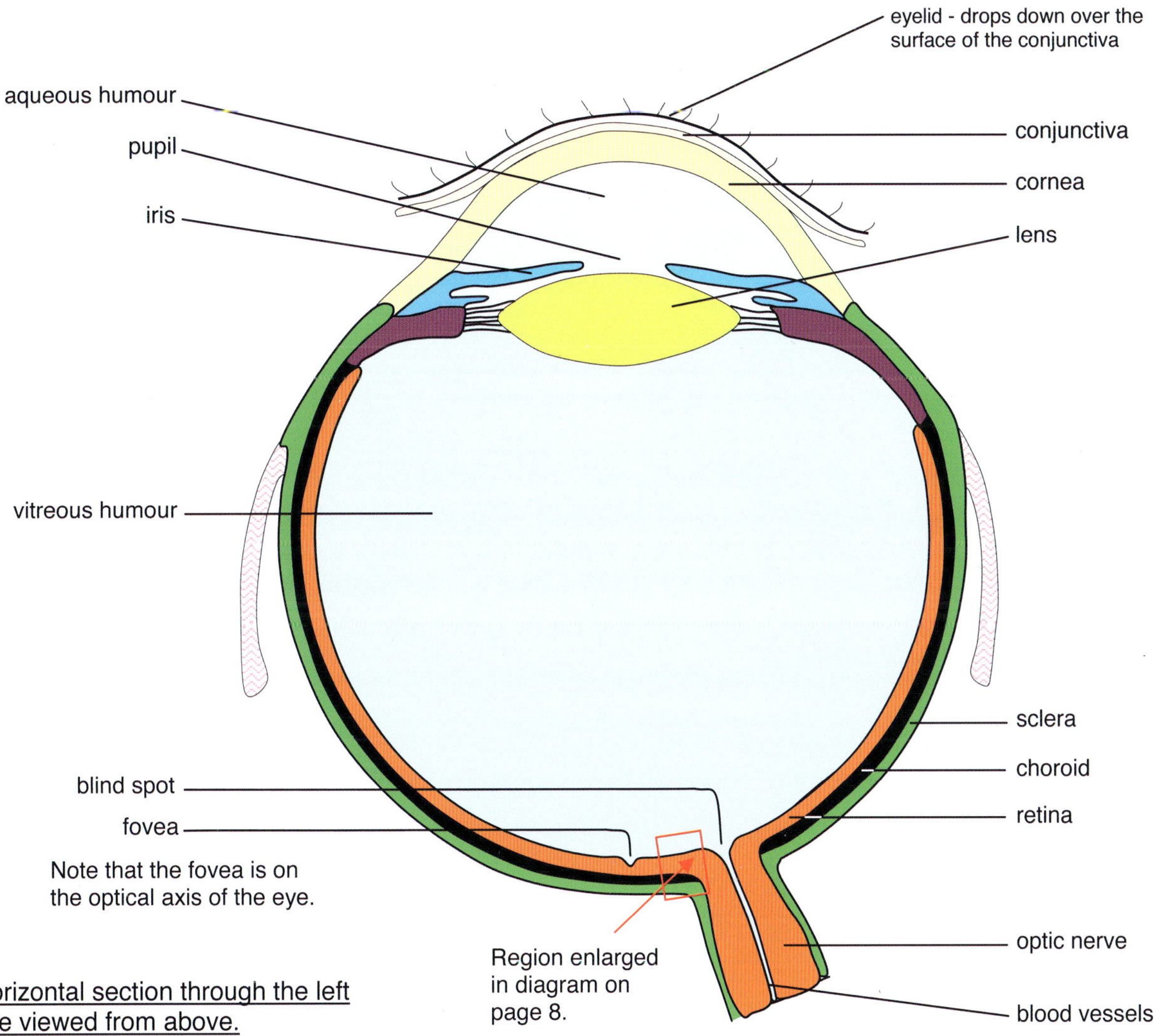

Note that the fovea is on the optical axis of the eye.

Horizontal section through the left eye viewed from above.

Rods and Cones

	Rods	Cones
Sensitivity	High – used in dim light.	Low – used in bright light.
Types	One type detects all wavelengths but in monochrome.	Three types absorbing maximally at blue, green and red regions of the spectrum.
Wiring	Connected in groups to a single neuron in the optic nerve.	Each connected to individual neuron in optic nerve.

Hint – rod = dim : cones = colour

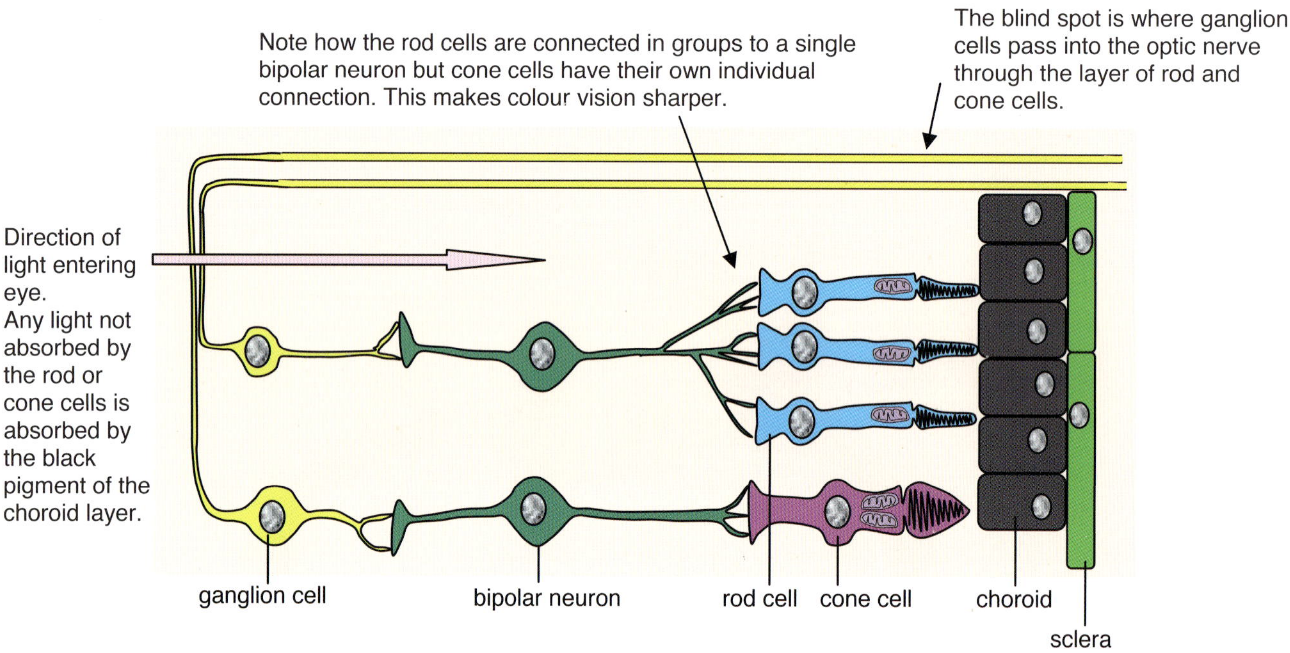

Find your blind spot
Hold the book in front of you about 50cm away. Close your left eye and look at the cross with your right eye. Slowly bring the book towards you. At around 35 – 40cm the blue spot will disappear. Try swinging your head from side to side still looking at the cross – you still won't be able to see the spot. Try the other way round as well.

Visual Processing

Contralateral processing

Key points

- Pigment molecules in the rods and cones detect the light stimulus;
- Bipolar neurons transfer electrical information from rod or cone cells to axons of ganglion cells;
- Left and right optic nerves meet at optic chiasma in brain;
- Axons from the half of the retina closest to the nose cross over to opposite side of brain;
- Thus information from the left visual field goes to right side of brain and vice versa;
- The visual cortex is arranged in columns of cells alternating left and right eyes;
- Cells at the border of columns receive input from both eyes. These are binocular cells;
- Binocular cells interpret distance by measuring the difference between where the same stimulus falls on the two retinas.

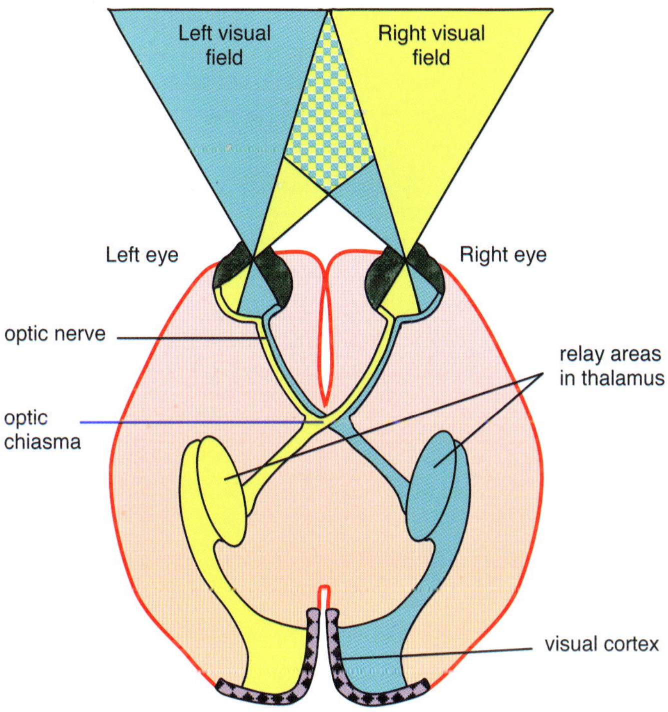

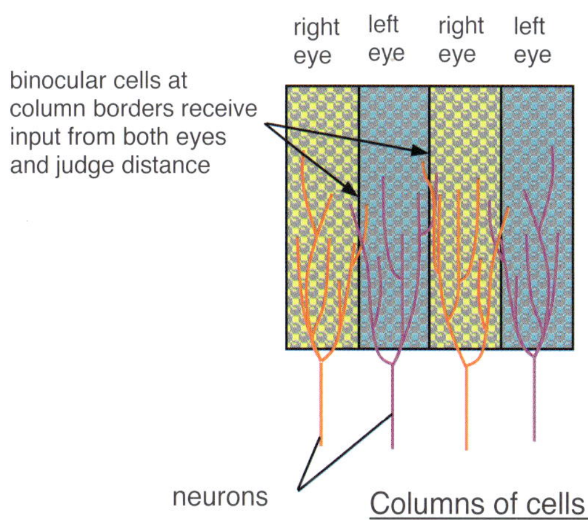

Columns of cells in the visual cortex.

Edge enhancement

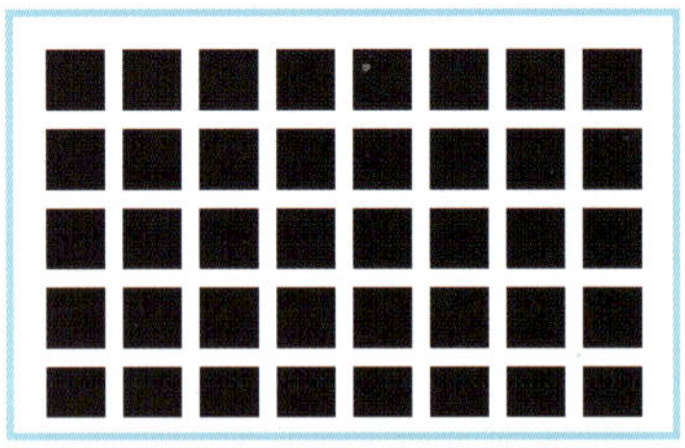

The Hermann grid illusion – notice how the street intersections contain a grey spot except where you look at an intersection directly.

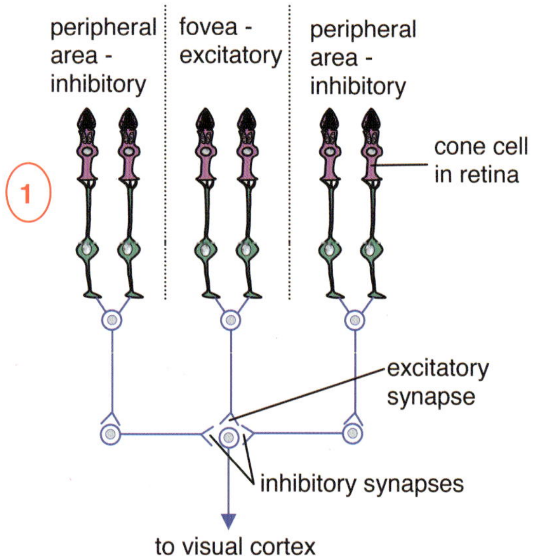

Explanation

- The grey spot is due to 'edge enhancement' or 'gain';
- Gain is like the brightness control on your computer screen;
- Cells in the retina adjust the brightness in a similar way;
- A difference is that the computer control alters the entire screen whereas in the retina it can do it in small sections;
- This allows you to see a wide range of both bright and dark detail in the same image;
- The size of these sections is determined by the spacing between the cones;
- The cones are tightly packed in the fovea but more widely spaced in the surrounding or peripheral area;
- When you look at a small object the image is focused in the fovea;
- Connections in the fovea are excitatory – see 1 above;
- Connections between cells in the peripheral area, called lateral connections, are inhibitory - see 1 above;
- These lateral connections allow the retina to determine the **edge** of a shape;
- Excitatory connections increase gain : inhibitory connections decrease gain;

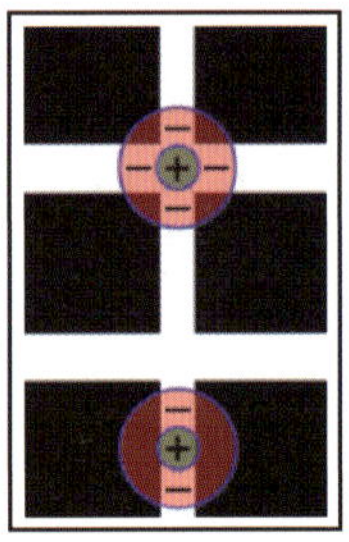

2

Now look at diagram 2;
- At an intersection the excitatory centre is surrounded by four inhibitory areas;
- On a street the excitatory centre has only two inhibitory areas;

Now look at diagram 3;
- If you look directly at an intersection (red circle) the image falls on the fovea. There is very little lateral inhibition and so you see it as white;
- On a street (green circle) there is a balance between light and dark areas and so no gain adjustment is needed;
- An intersection (blue circle) whose image falls on peripheral areas (inhibitory) means most of the image is flooded with white light and so the gain is turned down and that area appears grey.

3

There are two further examples in the Appendix on page 32.

Structure of The Human Ear

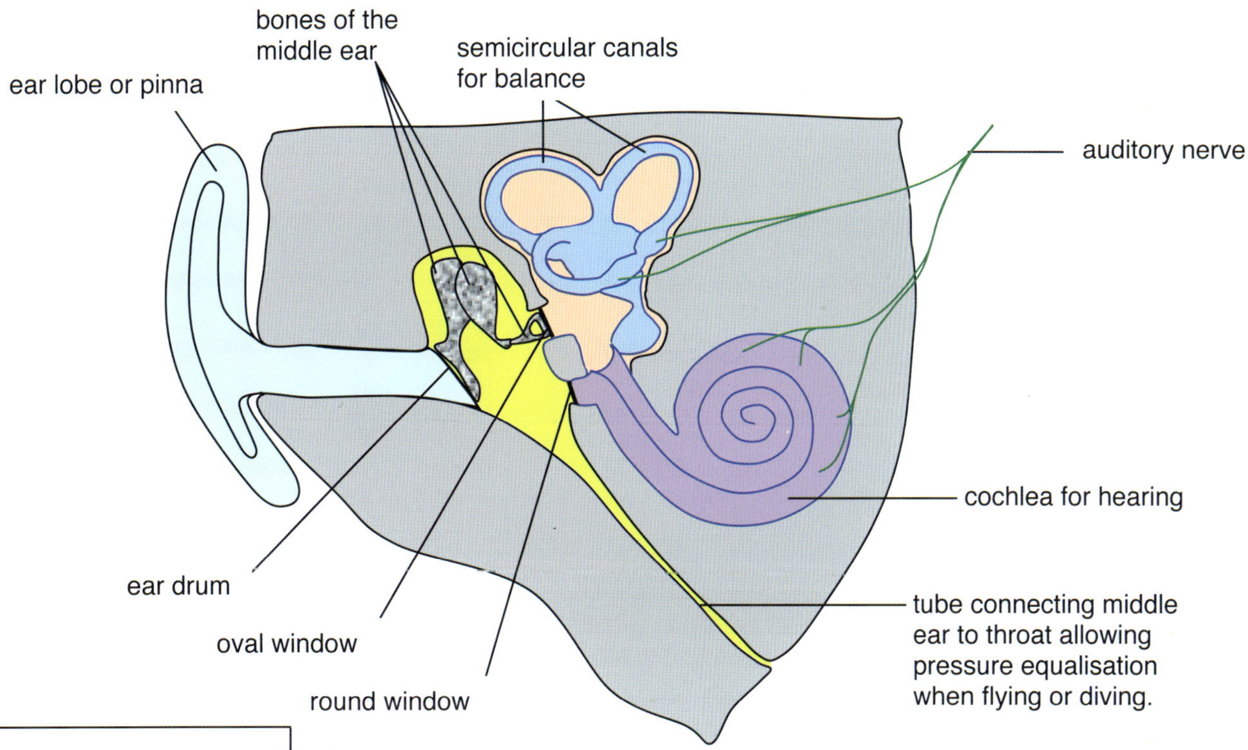

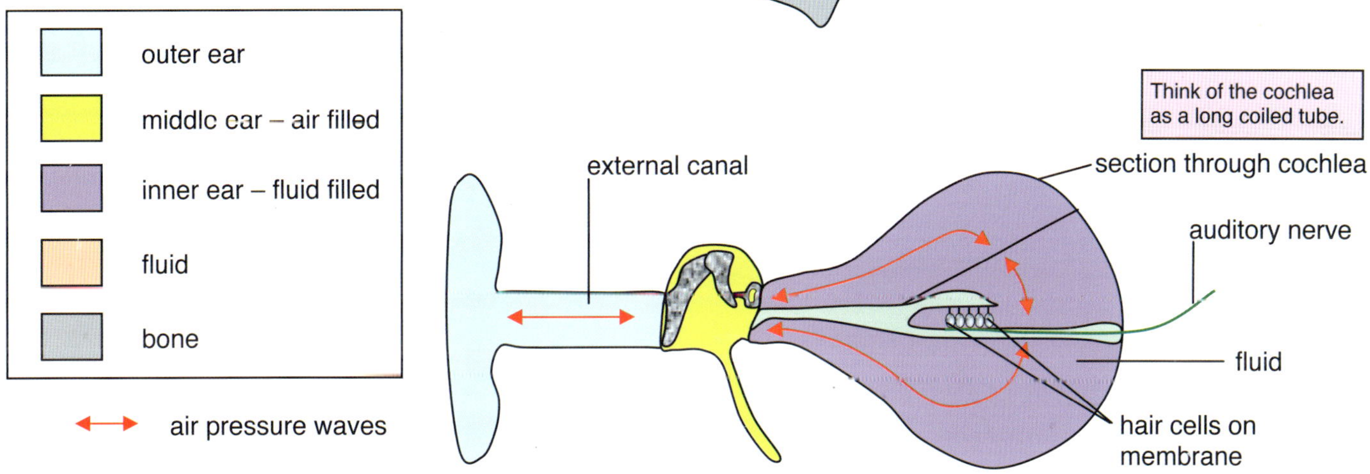

Key facts

- An air pressure wave passes down the external canal;
- This pushes on the **ear drum** which moves the **bones in the middle ear**;
- These bones have several functions –
  - the first bone is attached to the ear drum and the third to the oval window;
  - they act as levers which increases the force transmitted from the ear drum to the oval window;
  - muscles attaching them to the skull can contract as a result of a very loud sound and this prevents excessive movement of the oval window;
- The bones push on the **oval window** which causes a pressure wave in the fluid-filled cochlea;
- The **round window** moves in sympathy with the oval window, ie as the oval window moves in the round window moves out;
- This allows the fluid in the cochlea to move freely backwards and forwards;
- This fluid movement pushes on the membrane on which the **hair cells** sit;
- These hair cells are a type of mechanoreceptor; (see page 7)
- Movement of the hairs triggers nerve impulses in the auditory nerve;
- The pitch of a sound is determined by its frequency. Different frequencies travel different distances along the cochlea – the lower the frequency the further it travels;
- The louder the sound the greater the amplitude of the pressure wave and the greater the frequency of impulses sent to the brain.

Revision
Sensory Receptors

Complete the shaded boxes and dotted lines.

	Mechanoreceptors			
Stimulus	mechanical deformation	chemicals	temperature	light
Types		.... and .... receptors in the .... and on the	.... measures temperature of blood for temperature homeostasis.	

Revision
The Eye

Label the drawing of the eye.

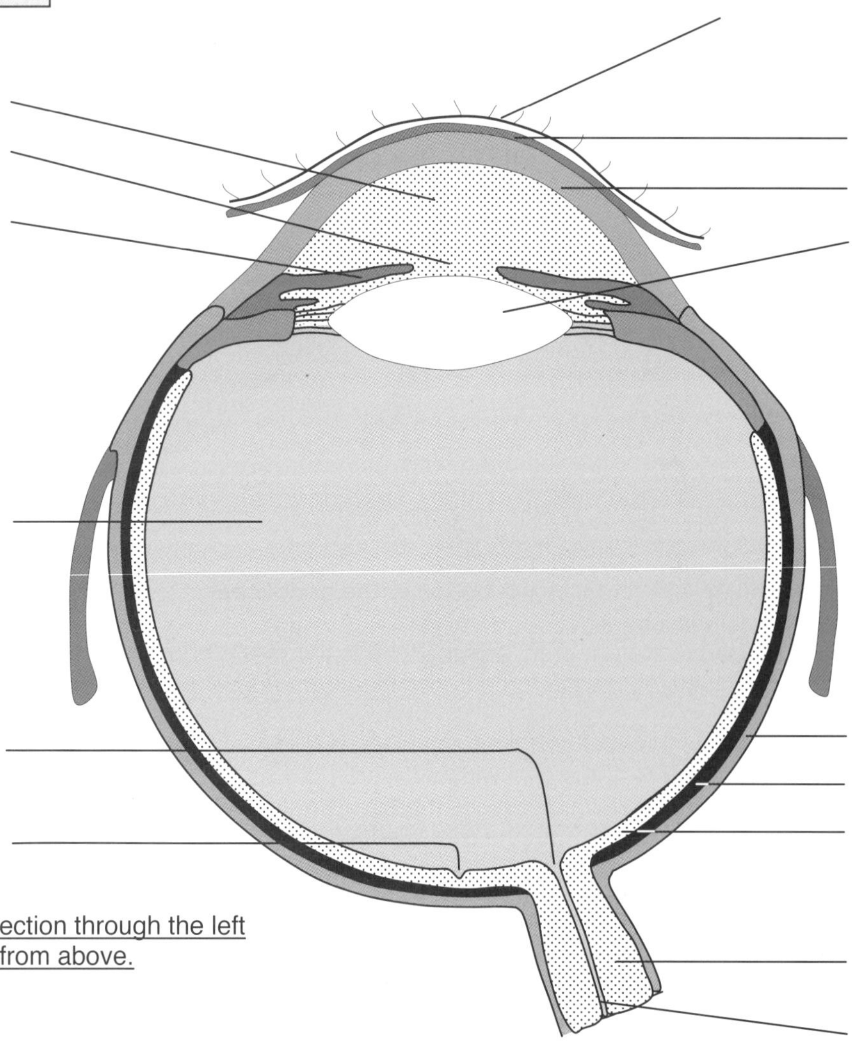

Horizontal section through the left eye viewed from above.

Revision
The Eye

Add relevant annotations in the three boxes and add labels on the dotted lines.

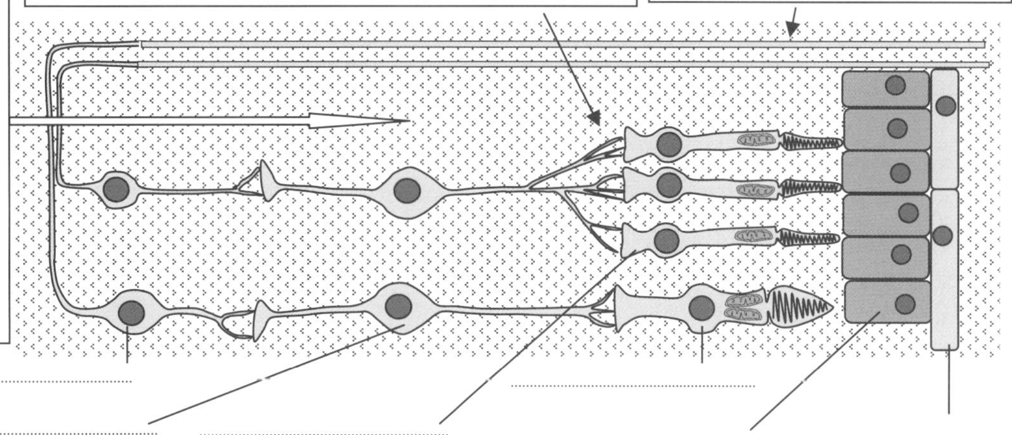

Distinguish between rods and cones.

Rods	Cones

Using the three numbered circles in the Hermann grid above explain the effect of edge enhancement.

Revision
The Ear

Label the drawing in the 6 places indicated.

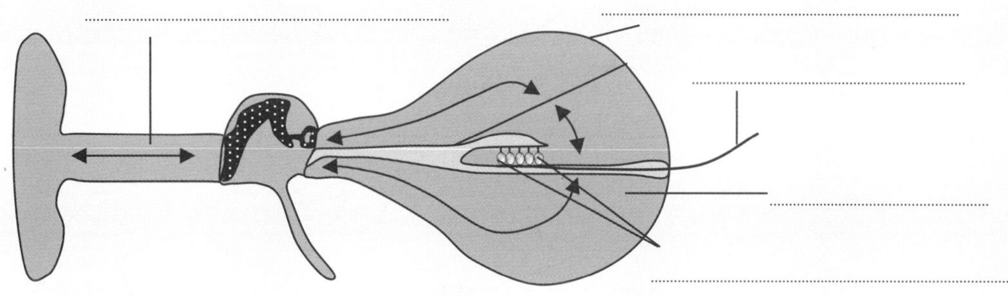

Revision
The Ear

Label the drawing in the 8 places indicated.

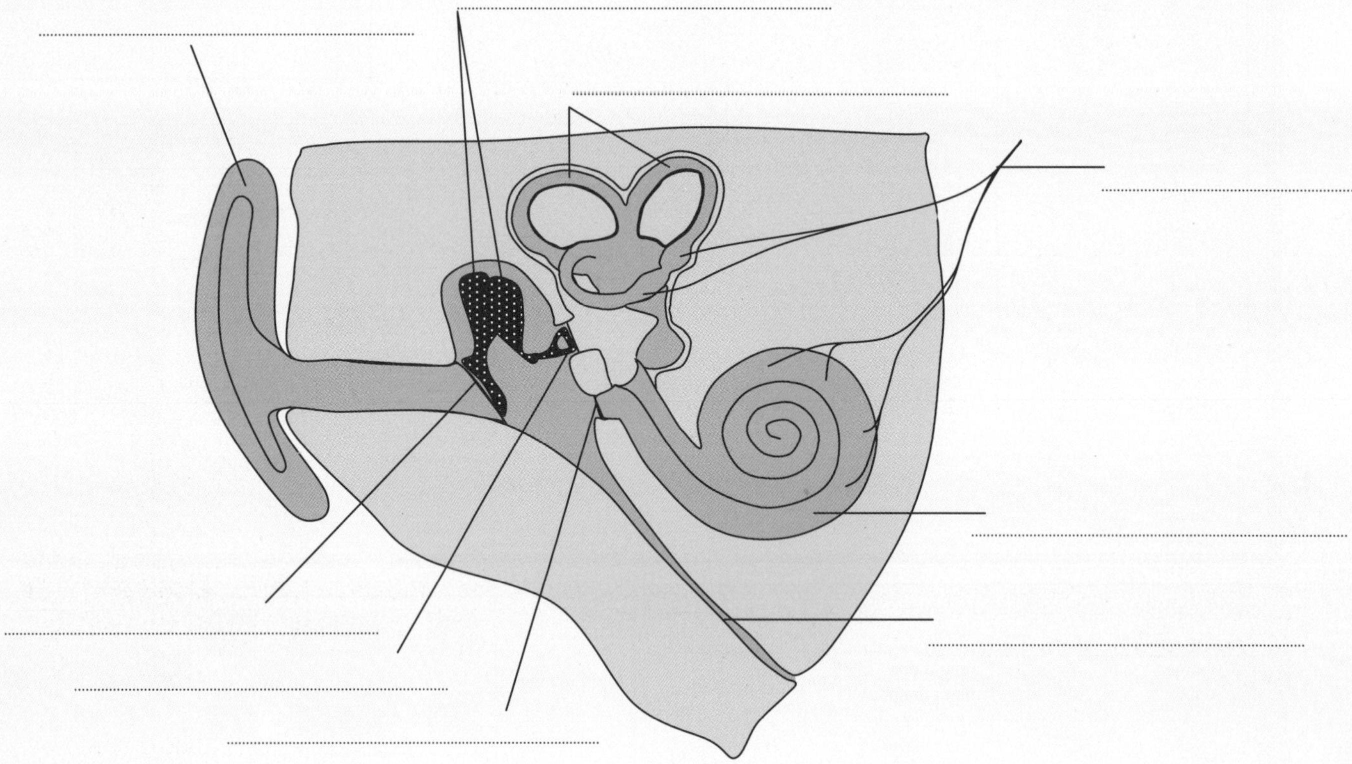

What is the role of the bones in the middle ear?

What is the role of the oval and round windows?

Outline how sound is detected in the cochlea.

❖ Innate and Learned Behaviour

Innate Behaviour
Behaviour that normally occurs in all members of a species despite natural variation in environmental influences.

Learned Behaviour
Behaviour developed as a result of experience, either by personal trial and error or from another individual.
There are several different types of learned behaviour. Classical conditioning is one – see page 16.

Kinesis
The movement of an organism in response to a stimulus such that rate of movement depends on intensity but not direction of stimulus.

This is innate behaviour. If an organism develops a behaviour pattern that improves its chances of survival and reproduction then that behaviour pattern will be selected by natural selection.

A woodlouse

The investigations below uses small invertebrates called woodlice.

A choice chamber investigation with woodlice.

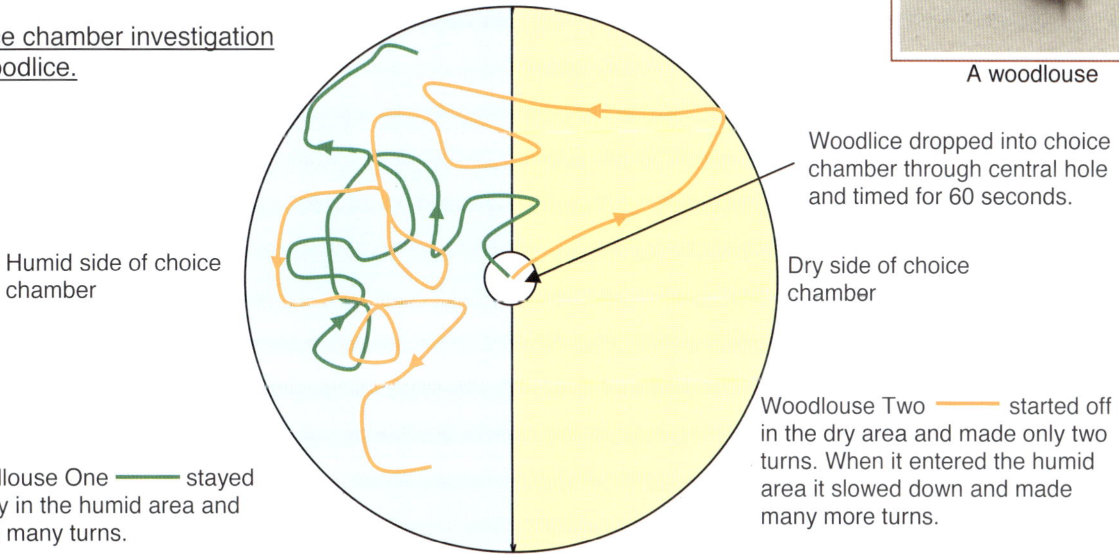

This is an example of kinesis. Gas exchange in woodlice is via external gills that need to be kept moist. In a dry area gas exchange could not take place and the woodlice would soon die. It is therefore advantageous to remain in a region that is humid.

Taxis
Locomotion of an organism in a particular direction in response to an external stimulus.
A positive response is towards the stimulus.
A negative response is away from the stimulus.

This is also innate behaviour. If the movement of an organism towards or away from a particular stimulus increases its chances of survival and reproduction then that movement will be selected by natural selection.

Woodlice can again be used for a taxis investigation. If 10 woodlice are dropped into the chamber above through the central hole then the number of woodlice on each side can be counted after 5 minutes.
Not surprisingly we would find that most woodlice have settled on the humid side.
The environment can easily be changed by making both sides humid, the preferred environment, and then making one side dark and one side light. The woodlice accumulate on the dark side because this is where they are less likely to be predated upon by birds.

Learned Behaviour and Survival

Points for discussion

- A greater range of behaviours can be acquired over time than could be acquired by natural selection;
- More complex behaviour can be developed over time which can confer great survival value for the species. By communication information can be passed on to later generations;
- Learning reduces the amount of non-adaptive behaviour, eg running into traffic, which increases the chances of survival;
- In higher organisms, eg primates, where there are many complex behaviours, it is very inefficient for each behaviour to be controlled by genes. It is much better to have a few genes which give the ability to learn;
- It allows behaviour to be tailored to a particular environment, eg a predator could switch to different forms of prey if its main source became scarce;
- Examples:-
    - An inexperienced caged Blue Jay bird will take a Milkweed butterfly if offered but spit it out due to its horrible taste. If offered another one it will refuse.
    - A horse will avoid touching an electric fence if it has experienced the shock from one. If moved to a new field with a mock-up of the same type of fence the horse will still avoid it even though it is not electrified.
    - Saddleback and Emperor Tamarins have a common predator and respond to each other's alarm calls;
    - Vervet monkeys have three different warning calls – leopard, snake and eagle. The young have to learn what type of response to make to each call. They also have to learn how to distinguish between an eagle (predator) and a vulture (harmless);
    - In dense African forest visual communication is difficult. Mongooses and several species of monkey, including Sooty Mangabey and Diana, hunt together and respond to each others warning calls. In this way there is a lookout at all levels from ground to canopy.

Classical Conditioning

> **Classical Conditioning**
> The modification of behaviour in an animal in response to a repeated stimulus such that the stimulus and response become associated.

Key points

- Also called Pavlovian conditioning after the Russian psychologist Pavlov who investigated saliva flow in dogs;
- He presented meat powder, the *unconditioned stimulus*, to the dog;
- The dog responded by increased saliva flow, the *unconditioned response*;
- He then rang a bell, at the same time as presenting the meat powder;
- After several repeats the bell alone, the *conditioned stimulus*, would cause the dog to increase saliva flow, the *conditioned response*.

Development of Birdsong - Latent Learning

Key points

- Adult songbirds have a species-specific song used in territorial display and courtship;
- In some species it is entirely innate but in others there is a part which is learned;
- Example – White-crowned sparrow, *Zonotrichia leucophrys*;
    - In nature the nestlings will hear the songs of mature males;
    - A young bird leaves the nest but does not become sexually mature until the following spring;
    - A male that has been hatched and reared in isolation can sing but not the species-specific song;

- Some components of what it sings are species-specific, indicating they are innate, but they are not the right length or in the right order.
- If a young bird hears the adult species-specific song it can then repeat that song the following spring;
- If a young bird hears the adult song but its hearing is blocked before spring it is unable to repeat the song;
- This means it has to hear its own singing and match what it hears with what was programmed into its memory as a young bird.
- If a young bird hears the adult song but its hearing is blocked after it has started to sing in the spring it is able to continue to repeat the song correctly even though it can no longer hear itself;
- Thus there are two learning phases in this bird:-
    - the first when it is young;
    - the second at the start of sexual maturity.

Distinguish between innate and learned behaviour.

State the meaning of either the term kinesis or the term taxis.

Outline an investigation of the term you have given above.

List 5 ways in which learning can improve the chance of survival.

State 2 examples of learning improving the chance of survival.

Outline Pavlov's investigations.

What is the name given to the type of response that Pavlov investigated?

In Pavlov's investigation what was the unconditioned stimulus?

In Pavlov's investigation what was the conditioned stimulus?

In Pavlov's investigation what was the unconditioned response?

In Pavlov's investigation what was the conditioned response?

State an example you could use for development of birdsong.

Outline the role of inheritance and learning in the development of birdsong using the example you have given in the box above.

❖ Neurotransmitters and Synapses

Decision making in the CNS

Some presynaptic neurons excite postsynaptic transmission and others inhibit postsynaptic transmission.

Key facts

- Synapses are junctions between neurons. (Revise core guide page 101);
- Each neuron has many synapses with other neurons;
- These synapses can be inhibitory or excitatory;

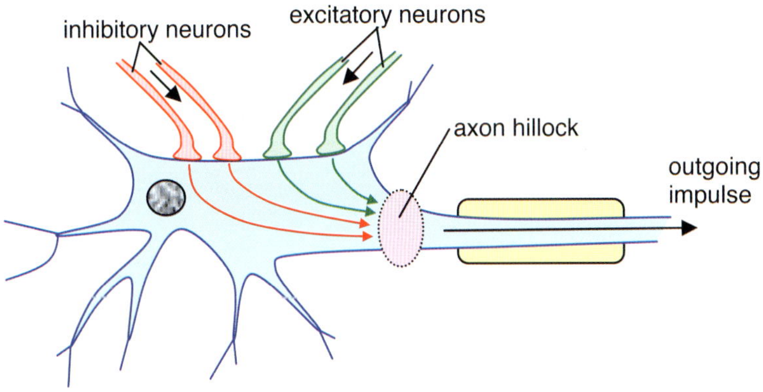

An action potential in the post synaptic neuron will only occur if the potential difference at the **axon hillock** rises above the threshold value.

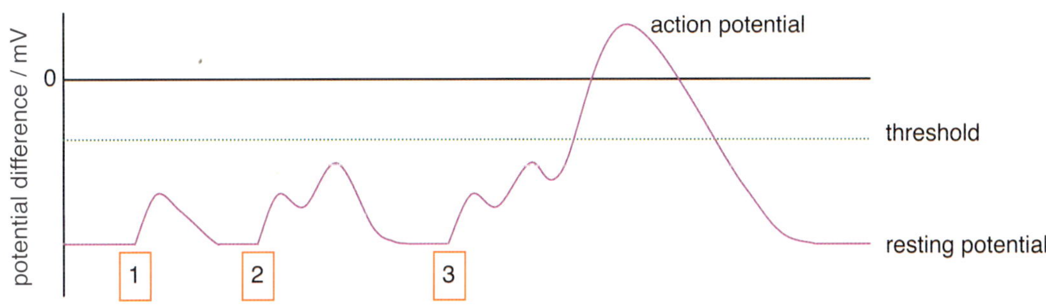

1 An impulse arrives through an excitatory neuron but the rise in potential difference is insufficient to reach the threshold and so an action potential does not occur.

2 Two excitatory impulses arrive close together and add up, but are still unable to reach the threshold and so an action potential does not occur.

3 Three presynaptic impulses arrive close together and add up, and this time do reach the threshold so an action potential does occur.

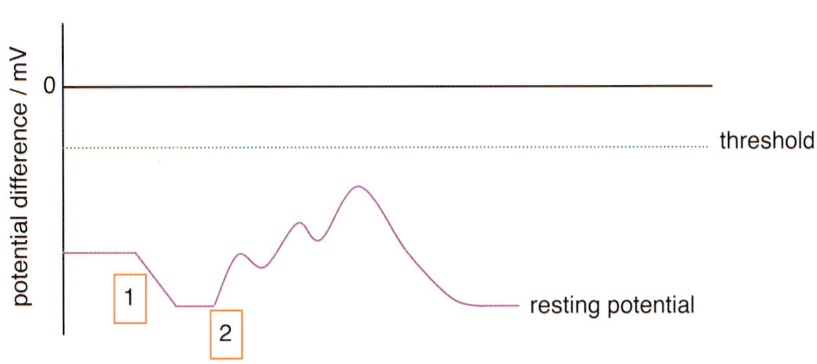

1 An impulse arrives through an inhibitory neuron and this makes the resting potential more negative due to a flow of negative chloride ions into the axon hillock.

2 The three rapid impulses that in the first diagram caused an action potential now have no effect as the threshold is not reached.

- Decisions are made by these multiple synapses;
- The effect of all the incoming impulses is summated at the axon hillock and if the threshold is reached then an action potential is produced.

- To illustrate this assume a value of at least +3 is required to initiate an action potential.
- Each inhibitory impulse contributes -1;
- Each excitatory impulse contributes +1.

example	inhibitory impulses	excitatory impulses	net value at axon hillock	action potential
1	0	2	+2	no
2	1	4	+3	yes
3	2	3	+1	no
4	2	6	+4	yes

Psychoactive drugs – the brain and personality

Key facts

- Drugs are chemicals which enter the body by breathing, injection, or eaten;
- They affect synaptic transmission;
- Their effects are shown in the diagram below;
- The effect can be stimulating or depressing – see table below.

Excitatory drugs :-
- Nicotine.
- Cocaine.
- Amphetamines.

Inhibitory drugs :-
- Benzodiazepines.
- Alcohol.
- Tetrahydrocannabinol – THC*

Mechanisms are in the numbered boxes

* THC is the active component in cannabis.

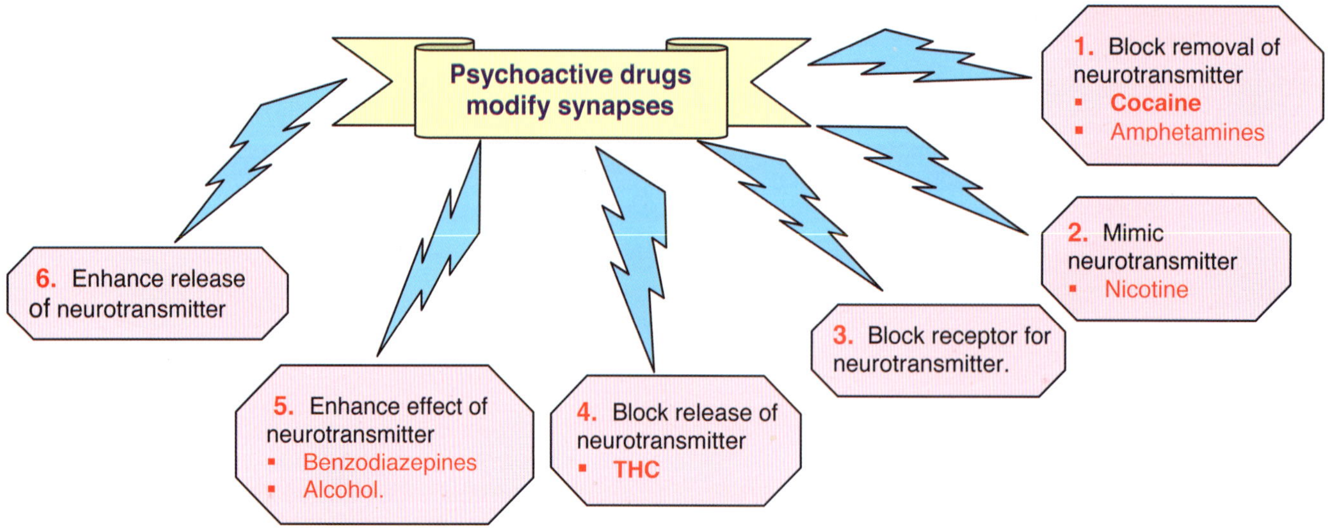

The actual effect is determined by whether the synapse is excitatory or inhibitory.

Drug action	Neurotransmitter	Result
Blocks	Excitatory	Depression
Enhances	Excitatory	Stimulation
Blocks	Inhibitory	Stimulation
Enhances	Inhibitory	Depression

Cocaine

- Source - leaves of the coca bush that grows in the Andes.
- Mechanism type 1 at dopaminergic synapses. (Reduces activity of the gene that makes the receptor.)
- Effects - Dopamine remains in synaptic gap; Increased energy and alertness; more talkative; constricts blood vessels; elevates body temperature; increases heart rate and blood pressure; increases pleasure feelings.
- Crack is a form of cocaine that can be heated to form a vapour. This is rapidly absorbed through the nasal capillaries; gives intense feelings of euphoria.
- Highly addictive. Gradually body makes less dopamine and so becomes dependent on presence of cocaine.

Tetrahydrocannabinol – THC

- Source – Hemp plant (Marijuana);
- Active ingredient is a compound called THC;
- Mechanism type 4 by blocking fusing of neurotransmitter vesicles with pre-synaptic membrane.
- Effects – Euphoria; relaxed inhibitions; increased appetite; dulling of pain; in higher doses produce psychedelic effects;
- May result in some psychological dependence.

Addiction

Points for discussion

Dopamine secretion

- Dopamine affects brain processes that control emotional response and feelings of pleasure;
- Thus anything that increases activity at dopamine synapses, and hence the feelings of pleasure, is likely to be repeated.

Social factors

- These can play a key role;
- Drugs may provide an 'escape' from poverty and social deprivation;
- Peer pressure in 'gangs';
- Cultural - used in a religious or shamanic context;
- People with mental health problems.

Genetic predisposition

- Susceptibility to drugs of any sort – nicotine, sleeping tablets, anti-depressants, psychoactive drugs - varies from person to person;
- Desensitisation to a drug, ie the effect from the same sized dose gets less and less, can take a long time in some people and in others a single dose is sufficient;
- There appear to be family traits;
- The above two points both imply a genetic component;
- Further research needs to be done to identify the genes involved;
- Results from the Human Genome Project may assist with this.

Neurotransmitters and Synapses

Decision making in the CNS is due to the effect of two types of presynaptic neuron. Name these.

Outline how impulses from these two types of presynaptic neuron affect the output of the postsynaptic neuron.

List two examples of excitatory psychoactive drugs excluding cocaine.

List two examples of inhibitory psychoactive drugs excluding THC.

How does cocaine affect synaptic transmission?

How does THC affect synaptic transmission?

List 4 other ways in which synaptic transmission can be affected by drugs.

State why dopamine secretion may lead to addiction.

List the social factors that may lead to addiction.

Extension material – HL only

❖ The Human Brain

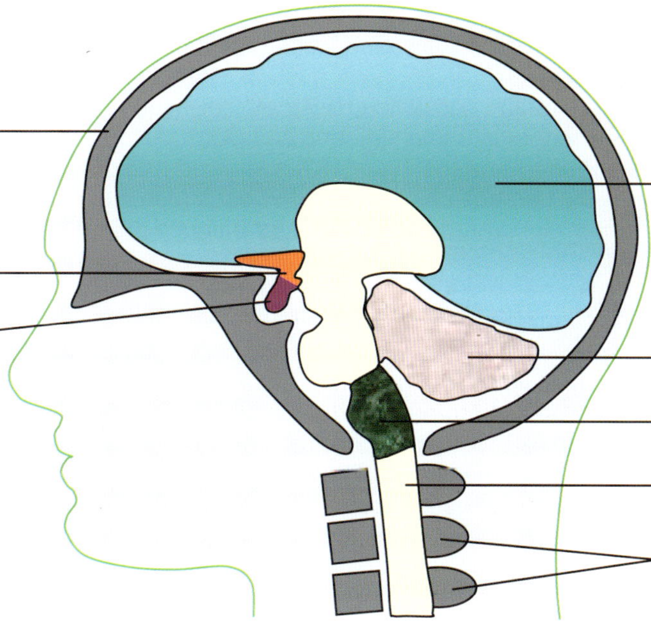

Region of brain	Function
Medulla oblongata	Regulatory centres for automatic and homeostatic activities - ▪ heart rate; ▪ breathing; ▪ blood pressure; ▪ swallowing; ▪ vomiting.
Cerebellum	Controls involuntary muscle movements for posture and balance.
Hypothalamus	Main control centre for autonomic nervous system (ANS); Co-ordinates ANS and endocrine systems – ▪ secretes the hormones that are stored in and released from the posterior pituitary; ▪ secretes the hormones (releasing factors) that control the anterior pituitary.
Pituitary gland	Divided into two regions. ▪ posterior lobe stores and releases hormones secreted by the hypothalamus; ▪ anterior lobe secretes hormones regulating many body functions.
Cerebral hemispheres	Integrating centre for high complex functions such as – ▪ learning; ▪ memory; ▪ emotions.

Investigating Brain Function

Key facts

Animal Experiments

- Usually involves surgery to remove part of the skull to access brain;
- Animal must be alive;
- Different regions of the brain are stimulated and the response of the animal observed;
- Primates were often used which raised ethical issues given their genetic similarity to humans and the pain and suffering caused;
- Example – Pierre Flourens in the 1820s showed that removing thin slices of tissue from the cerebellum of rabbits and birds resulted in the animals displaying a lack of muscular co-ordination and poor balance but no other obvious effects.

Lesions

- A lesion is a damaged part of the brain;
- This may be dues to a stroke, tumour, accident or deliberate injury;
- The change in ability of the person or experimental animal before and after lesion formation can be used to deduce the function of that region;
- The lesion may be produced by drilling a hole in the skull of the anaesthetised animal, inserting an electrode into a specific part of the brain and using an electric impulse to destroy the tissue around the electrode tip;
- Example – in rats a lesion in a specific part of the hypothalamus causes over-eating whereas a lesion in a different part caused the rats, initially, to refuse all food;
- Lesions in humans have been done for therapeutic purposes – certain nerve fibres linking opposite sides of the brain have been cut in an attempt to reduce epileptic seizures.

Functional Magnetic Resonance Imaging (FMRI)

- The FMRI scanner detects differences in oxygenated and deoxygenated blood;
- It can detect active brain tissue of only a few square mm;
- Brain tissue becomes active when stimulated and oxygen consumption increases;
- Change in oxygen consumption in the active neural area occurs 1-5 seconds after stimulus;
- Example – shown on the right.

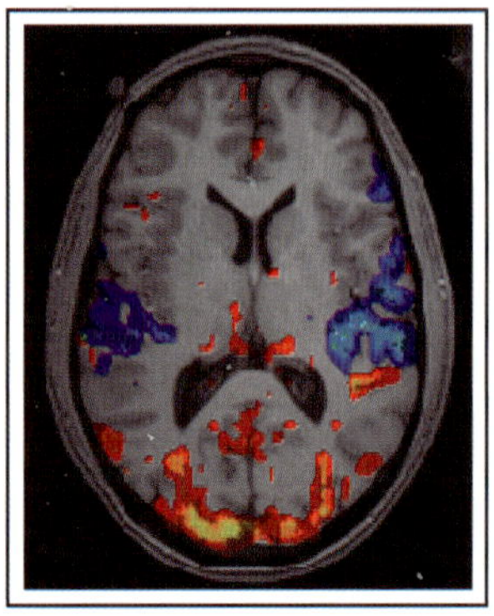

While lying in the FMRI scanner the subject watched a screen which alternated between showing a visual stimulus and being dark every 30 seconds.

Steve Smith
FMRI Centre
Department of Clinical Neurology
University of Oxford

The Autonomic Nervous System

The autonomic nervous system (ANS) consists of sympathetic and parasympathetic motor neurons.

The roles of the sympathetic and parasympathetic systems are largely antagonistic.

The ANS in relation to the nervous system as a whole

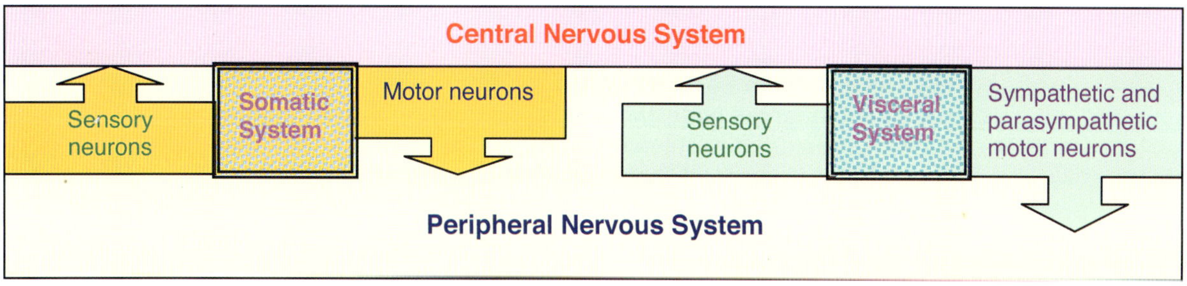

The somatic system is largely conscious and deals mainly with surface receptors and the skeletal muscles.

The visceral system is largely subconscious and deals with systems such as heart, gut, breathing. The motor neurons of the visceral system form the ANS.

	Sympathetic	Parasympathetic
Heart	Increases rate during fright or excitement to supply more blood (oxygen and glucose) to muscles.	Decreases rate during rest and sleep.
Gut	Decreases blood flow so more can be diverted to skeletal muscles.	Increases blood flow.
Iris	Dilates pupil by contracting radial iris muscles to improve the image.	Constricts pupil to protect retina by contracting circular iris muscles.

These things happen when you get frightened – heart beats faster, eyes get wider, 'sinking' feeling in your stomach. This is because the neurotransmitter at sympathetic synapses is noradrenaline, which has the same effect as the hormone adrenaline.

The body is being prepared for action.

The Pupil Reflex

Key points

- Protects retina from damage by excess light;
- Allows sufficient light in for vision;
- Impulses from retina are monitored for intensity by the brain stem;
- The higher the intensity the higher the frequency of impulses; (The brain stem is a part of the brain that includes the medulla oblongata);
- Motor impulses sent to radial or circular iris muscles to change diameter of pupil;
- A bright light causes the circular muscles to contract and the pupil decreases in diameter;
- Both eyes respond even if only one eye is stimulated.

The Pupil Reflex and Brain Death

Key point

- Failure of the pupil reflex in an unconscious casualty probably means brain death and the casualty is not likely to recover.
- This is because it indicates that if the brain stem is damaged the medulla oblongata is also probably damaged.
- The medulla oblongata regulates the basic life functions of breathing and heart rate.

Sensing Pain

Key points

- Pain receptors are free nerve endings;
- Located throughout body and especially where damage is most likely to occur;
- Sensitive to extremes of temperature, intense mechanical stimulation or specific chemicals in tissue fluid, including some released by injured cells;
- Fast pain receptors provide immediate sensation of pain to allow rapid response;
- Slow pain receptors continue feeling of pain. These can be controlled – see below.

Natural Painkillers

Key points

- Nerve impulses from the brain cause endorphins from the hypothalamus and pituitary to be released into the blood;
- Endorphin receptors are found in many places in the central nervous system;
- When endorphins bind to their receptors they block the sensation of pain;
- They also produce the pleasant feelings associated with vigorous activity.

Revision
The Brain

Add labels where there are lines.

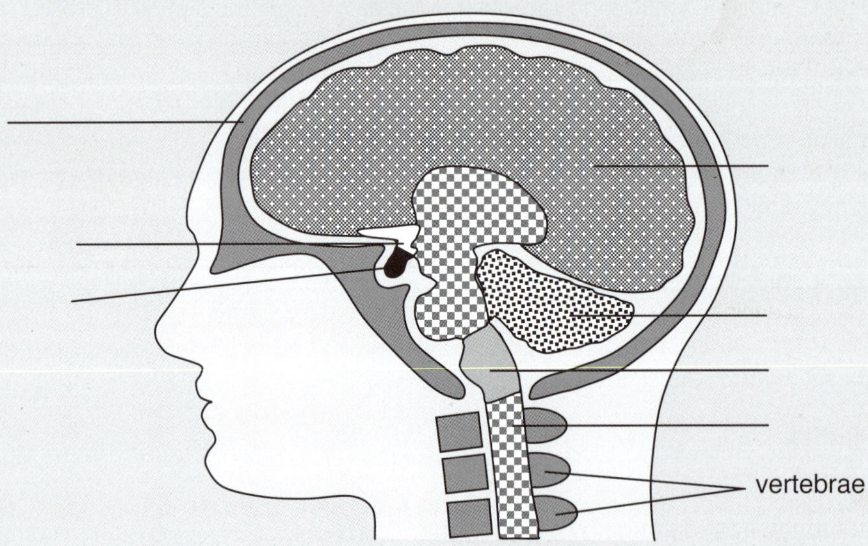

What is the function of the pupil reflex?

Why is the absence of the pupil reflex a good indication of brain death?

Describe how endorphins act as painkillers.

Revision
Functions of the Brain

Complete the shaded boxes and the 4 dotted lines.

Region of brain	Function
	Regulatory centres for the autonomic nervous system - ▪ heart rate; ▪ .... ▪ ....
	Controls involuntary muscle movements for posture and....................................
Hypothalamus	Main control centre for autonomic nervous system – ▪ ....
	Secretes many hormones - ▪ ones having a direct effect eg ▪ ones regulating other endocrine glands eg
Cerebral hemispheres	

Outline how animal experiments have been used to determine brain function?

What is a lesion of the brain?

How are lesions helpful in determining brain function?

Outline how FMRI scanning is used in identifying specific regions of the brain.

Revision
Effects of the ANS

Complete the shaded boxes.

	Sympathetic	Parasympathetic
Heart		
Blood flow to the gut		
Iris		

❖ Further Studies of Behaviour

Social Organisation of the Honey Bee *Apis mellifera*

Key points

Three castes -

- One queen;
  - fertilised by drone;
  - egg laying;
  - produces several different pheromones to regulate the activities of the workers.
- 200 – 1000 drones (males);
  - produced from unfertilised eggs;
  - mate with virgin queen to continue colony;
  - old queen plus some workers then leave to found a new colony.
- 50,000 workers – sterile females;
  - produced from fertilised eggs;
  - days 3 to 4 – cleaning;
  - days 5 to 20 – house bee doing a range of jobs – guard duty, temperature and humidity control, cell building from secreted wax, feeding larvae, processing honey;
  - days 21 to 40 – foraging for nectar and pollen;
  - also produce pheromones to help co-ordinate activities;
  - around 6 different pheromones are involved.

Social Organisation of the Army Ant *Eciton burchelli*

A major worker.*

A submajor worker *

* Reproduced with the kind permission of the photographer Alex Wild.

- Found in South America;
- This species is a nomadic swarm raider and make temporary nests or bivouacs;
- The walls of the bivouac are made from the ants themselves and inside are chambers and corridors;
- There are three hierarchies – a single queen, workers and soldiers;
- The workers are subdivided into larger ones foraging and smaller ones tending the queen and the brood;
- Reproduction is cyclic;
- When the larvae start to pupate they are moved to edge of the bivouac and eggs are laid by the queen and arranged in the centre of the bivouac;
- When the eggs hatch chemical signals stimulate the nightly nomadic swarming phase in order to provide sufficient food;
- Raids can be 15 metres across and contain over 100,000 ants moving in a very organised way – a swarm in front and a fan of columns behind where the ants tear up and prepare the prey to be carried back;
- These columns are protected by the soldiers;
- They feed on arthropods and small vertebrates;
- The queen co-ordinates activities within the colony with pheromones.

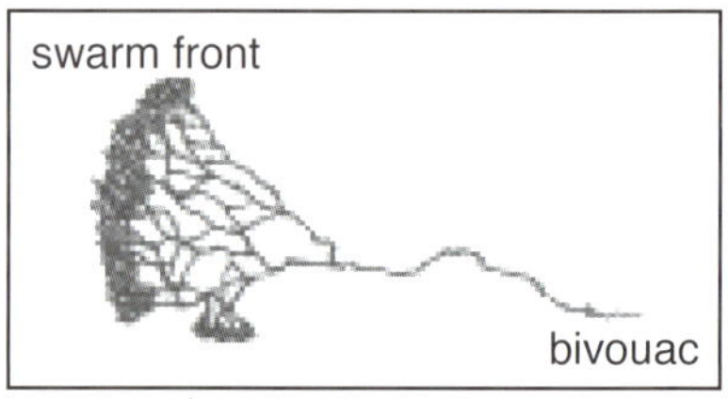

Social organisation and natural selection

Key points

- Members of the colony work for the benefit of the colony and not themselves;
- Co-operation of individuals ensures survival of the colony;
- The more efficient this co-operation the more likely the colony is to survive;
- Thus natural selection will act at the level of the colony.

Altruistic Behaviour

Altruism is behaviour that gives no advantage to the individual, and may in fact be disadvantageous, but benefits another individual which may or may not be related.

Points for discussion

Florida Scrub Jay

- This is a bird found in the drier shrub areas of Florida;
- Shows altruistic behaviour for a short time;
- Offspring of a pair from the previous breeding season help to feed the next brood, defend the territory and watch for predators;
- They remain non-reproductive till next breeding season;
- Nests with helpers have more offspring than those that don't;
- Helpers share genes with new brood so being altruistic increases chances of shared genes passing to later generations.

Florida scrub jay *Aphelocoma coerulescens* Photo reproduced by kind permission of the photographer Paul J Willoughby.

Vampire bats

- Found in Central and South America;
- Form social groups, colonies, of unrelated individuals;
- Nocturnal feeders on fresh blood from animals such as horses and cattle;
- The chance of failing to feed successfully is quite high;
- Bats failing to find food on two consecutive nights usually die of starvation;
- If a bat returns to the colony hungry other, unrelated bats feed it;
- A bat that has been fed in this way will give food at another time;
- Because the risk of failing to feed is quite high it is beneficial for a well fed bat to give food to a hungry bat since another time it may fail to feed and could die if it did not receive food from another bat;
- This is called reciprocal altruism;
- An important difference with the Florida Scrub Jay is that the individuals involved may not be genetically related.

Vampire bat

Foraging Behaviour and Food Optimisation

Bluegill fish (*Lepomis macrochirus*) feeding on Daphnia

Bluegill fish. Photo James F. Parnell

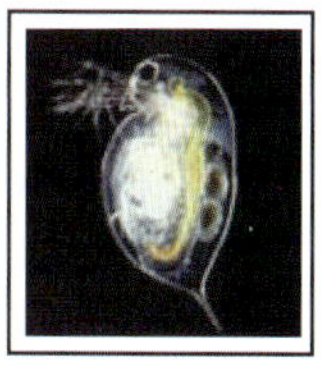

Daphnia. Photo: Paul Hebert

Key facts

- Daphnia are small fresh water crustaceans that are born fully formed and grow larger;
- This gives the fish a choice of sizes;
- At low Daphnia numbers the fish eat all sizes in order to gain enough energy;
- As Daphnia numbers increase the fish become more and more selective and eat an increasing proportion of the larger ones;
- This optimises the energy intake for the energy expenditure.

Oystercatchers (*Haematopus ostralegus*) feeding on limpets (*Patella* spp.)

Key facts

- Limpets inhabit rocky shores and when covered by water graze on algae;
- As the tide goes out the limpets return to their home site which is shaped to fit their shell;
- They prevent desiccation by clamping onto the rock;

Oystercatcher on the Llyn Peninsular. Photo Alan Gray

Further Studies

Limpets

- They can be solitary or rest in clusters;
- It was found that oystercatchers preferred to attack solitary limpets rather than those in clusters;
- There was no nutritional or size differences between solitary and clustered limpets;
- Oystercatchers preferred to attack the anterior end of the limpet;
- This anterior end was more exposed to the angle of attack in a solitary limpet because when clustered neighbouring limpets often prevented this preferred attack angle;
- When one limpet in a cluster was attacked the other limpets responded by clamping down more tightly making it very difficult for the oystercatcher to remove them;
- Thus the oystercatcher expended less energy by attacking solitary limpets.

Mate Selection and Exaggerated Traits

The Blue bird of paradise, *Paradisaea rudolphi*

(Photographer unknown)

Key facts

- Birds of paradise, found on the island of New Guinea, show extremes of exaggerated traits;
- Only the males show these traits;
- The bright feathers and displays make the birds very obvious to predators, could hinder their escape and make searching for food more difficult;
- Thus an individual that is in good condition and able to display is likely to be very strong;
- These characteristics would be genetic;
- A female selecting such an individual is therefore selecting strong genes;
- The females must also have genes that select for these exaggerated traits;

The Lesser bird of paradise *Paradisaea minor*

Reproduced with the kind permission of the photographer Robert Joyon.

Rhythmical Behaviour Patterns

Animals show rhythmical variations in activity.

Key facts

Such behaviour patterns could be over short periods of time such as a few hours or 24 hours, or longer such as a year, or even over many years;
The behaviour may be associated with feeding or reproduction;
Example 1

- Marbled Duck, *Marmaronetta angustirostris*.
- Predated on by day-hunting birds of prey such as buzzards;
- The duck is therefore mainly a nocturnal feeder;
- In the day they remain hidden in reed beds.

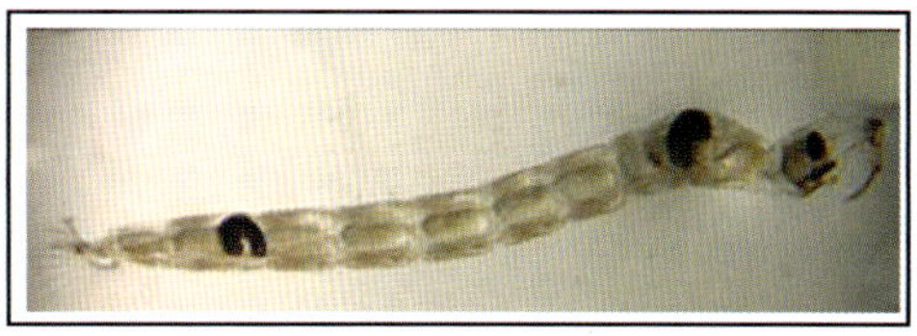

Example 2

- Phantom midge, *Chaoborus punctipennis*;
- This is a non-biting fly similar to a mosquito;
- The larvae are voracious predators of small zooplankton in aquatic ecosystems;
- They are themselves predated on by fish;
- They burrow 1 to 2cm into the soft mud sediments at sunrise to avoid day feeding fish;
- Towards sunset they move up to the water/mud interface and when the light intensity is low enough emerge into the water to feed;
- As day length changes in the summer this upward migration through the mud changes so that the larvae always reach the water/mud interface at sunset;
- Light cannot penetrate into the mud so this must be a diurnal rhythm which is reset every day upon arrival at the mud surface;
- This rhythmic behaviour within the mud maximizes the amount of time they can spend feeding in the water.

Outline the social organisation of a honey bee colony.

How does foraging behaviour optimise food intake in bluegill fish?

How does mate selection lead to exaggerated traits? Give an example.

What is meant by the term altruism?

State the key points about evolution of altruism in the Florida Scrub Jay.

What is the value of the diurnal rhythmic behaviour of phantom midge, *Chaoborus,* larvae within the mud?

Appendix

This is the reverse of the Hermann grid, ie white squares and black streets. The result though is just the same with grey spots at the intersections.

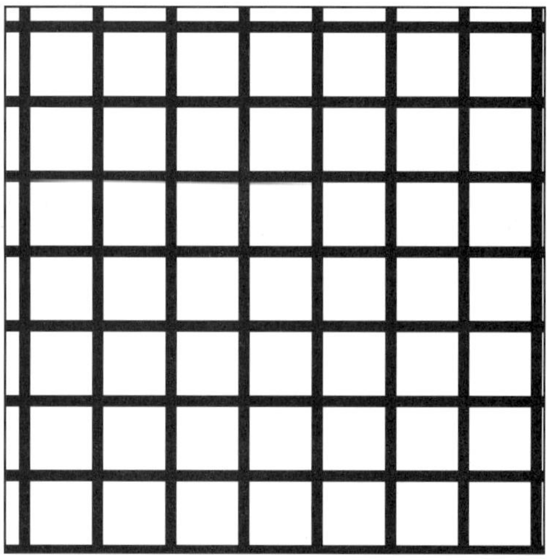

A similar but more powerful illusion, known as the *Lingelbach illusion* or the *scintillating grid illusion*, was discovered in 1994 by Elke Lingelbach, the wife of a German mathematics professor, and has not yet been fully explained.

As you move your eyes over the grid black spots briefly appear in the white circles but only in the peripheral areas.

Curiously, the effect of the scintillation is lessened by tilting the head through 45°!